CONTENTS

West Africa and its Food

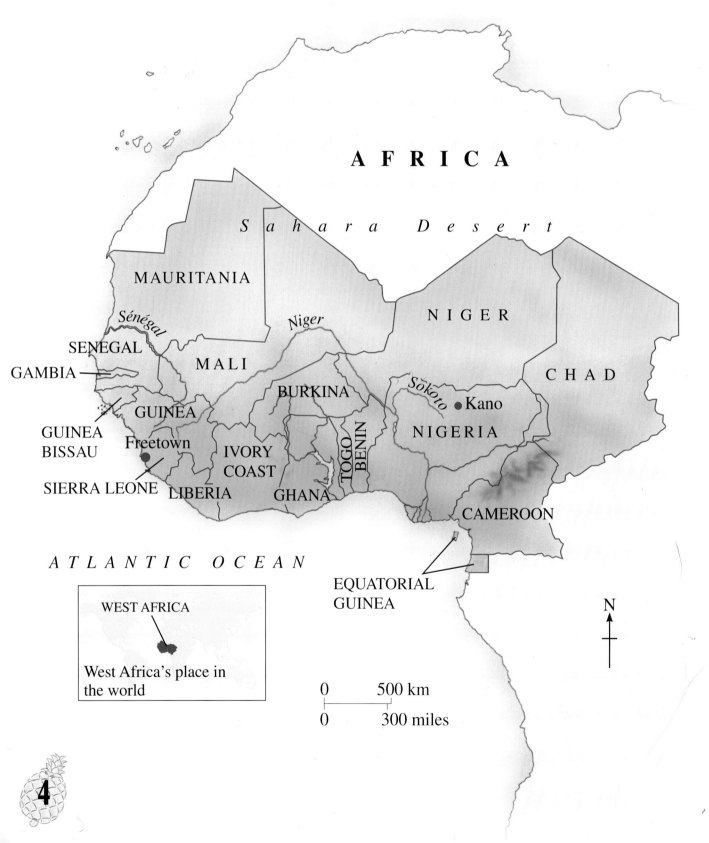

AFRICA

Sahara Desert

MAURITANIA

Sénégal

Niger

NIGER

SENEGAL

GAMBIA

MALI

CHAD

Sokoto

BURKINA

GUINEA

• Kano

GUINEA
BISSAU

Freetown

NIGERIA

IVORY
COAST

SIERRA LEONE

TOGO

BENIN

LIBERIA

GHANA

CAMEROON

ATLANTIC OCEAN

EQUATORIAL
GUINEA

N

WEST AFRICA

West Africa's place in
the world

| 0 | 500 km |
| 0 | 300 miles |

Millet and corn

Millet and corn are both grain crops, like rice. Grain crops are one of the main foods for most people in West Africa.

Fish

Fish and seafood are an important source of protein for people who live near a coast or river.

Yams and cassava

Yams and cassava are the other main foods in West Africa. They are both root vegetables, which means that they grow underground.

Peanuts

Peanuts, which are also called groundnuts, are really a type of bean. They are a main food crop in the dry north.

Cattle, sheep and goats

These animals are mainly kept for their milk. Farmers in the north move their cattle around in herds, and sell them for meat.

Fruit

Fruits such as mangoes, coconuts, pineapples and bananas grow on plantations, as well as in the wild.

Food and Farming

West Africa is a vast region in Africa, made up of seventeen different countries. Over 182 million people live there. West Africa has many different landscapes. In the south, along the coast, it is hot and rainy all year round. Here, thick rain forests cover the land. Further north, where the climate is drier, there are grassy plains and deserts. The climate of West Africa affects the type of food that is grown.

▼ In dry Mauritania, two nomads milk a camel.

Millet, corn and rice

Millet and corn are two of the main foods in West Africa. Millet grows easily in the drier, northern areas of West Africa. Corn (which is also known as maize) needs more water than millet, so it grows further south. Both corn and millet are usually pounded into flour and used to make porridge and cakes. Rice only grows in the wetter south of the region, or near rivers.

▼ These women in Mali are winnowing millet.

Yams, cassava and groundnuts

The most important vegetables in West Africa are yams, cassava and groundnuts (peanuts). Yams and cassava are both root crops, like potatoes. Their thick, white roots are either peeled or grated before they are cooked. Sometimes yams are pounded into *fufu*, which is a bit like mashed potato. Cassava must be cooked properly, because it is poisonous if it is eaten raw.

Groundnuts grow easily in the dry north. They were brought here from South America by the Portuguese, over 500 years ago.

This boy is grating ▶ cassava in Ghana.

◄ This girl is looking after her family's goats, in Ghana.

Chickens, goats and cattle

Most West African farmers have a few goats or chickens. Goats and cattle are mainly kept for their milk. Chickens are kept for their meat and for their eggs.

Women cleaning ► groundnuts in Senegal. Groundnuts grow underground, so they have to be cleaned before they are eaten or turned into oil.

FISH FESTIVALS

The lively fish festival of Argungu takes place on the Sokoto river in Nigeria every year. The men have a competition to see who can catch the biggest fish. They use calabashes and nets, which are traditional fishing tools. The winners receive prizes, usually money.

▲ The Hausa people of Nigeria take part in the Argungu fish festival.

Fish

Fish and seafood are important foods for people who live near the coast, or near rivers such as the Senegal or the Niger. These foods contain protein, which helps the body to grow. Fish is often smoked over a fire to preserve it. Since fish is quite expensive, many people eat it only on special occasions.

People and religions

People in West Africa come from many different backgrounds, with their own languages, religions and traditions. This is because people have come to West Africa from other countries over hundreds of years, bringing their religions and customs with them. These have influenced the food and festivals in West Africa today.

Many people in West Africa, especially in the north and west, are Muslims. They follow the religion of Islam. In Senegal and the Gambia, 90 per cent of the people are Muslims.

▼ These guards, in northern Nigeria, are Muslims. They work for the emir, who is the local ruler.

Ramadan and Id-ul-Fitr

The month of Ramadan is the most holy occasion in the Muslim religion. During this month, every year, most Muslims do not eat any food or drink between sunrise and sunset. They do this to obey the Muslim holy book, called the Qur'an, and to remind themselves that all food comes from Allah.

Fasting during the day for a whole month is quite a difficult thing to do. Children under the age of about twelve, pregnant women and the sick and elderly do not have to take part in the fast.

▼ Praying to Allah at the end of Ramadan, in Cameroon.

Id-ul-Fitr

In the Muslim calendar, the months do not begin and end on fixed dates. Instead, a new month begins when the new moon appears. When the Imam (the religious leader of a town or area) spots the new moon at the end of Ramadan, it is time for the festival of Id-ul-Fitr to begin.

The festival begins with the beating of a drum. Everyone dresses in their best clothes and goes to the mosque to say their prayers. They pray on special prayer mats, or colourful rugs.

FORBIDDEN FOOD

In the Muslim holy book, the Qur'an, certain foods are forbidden. No Muslims are allowed to eat pork.

▼ These men in Nigeria are beating different types of drum.

13

▲ This street procession is held at the start of Id-ul-Fitr, in the city of Kano, Nigeria.

Processions and presents

There are processions through many villages at Id-ul-Fitr. In northern Nigeria there is a huge, colourful parade called a *sallah*. People crowd through the streets to the emir's palace. There, men on horseback charge forward to salute the emir.

An important part of Id-ul-Fitr is giving to the poor. People also visit friends and give presents of sweets. Eating, drinking and dancing goes on throughout the night, and the celebrations can last for several days.

Tobaski
(Id-ul-Adha)

The festival of Tobaski, or Id-ul-Adha, is another important celebration for Muslims in West Africa. It marks the time when Allah tested the prophet Abraham by asking him to kill his own son. He only stopped Abraham at the last moment. Abraham sacrificed a sheep instead.

Today at Tobaski, there is a special feast. The head of the household slaughters a goat or a sheep, which is eaten at the meal. Sometimes it is cooked in a peanut sauce, or with vegetables such as aubergines or cassava.

▲ Snacks of small fish pies, doughnuts and popcorn are prepared for visitors on special occasions in the Gambia.

This man has bought ▶ a goat at a market in the Gambia, for the feast of Tobaski.

▲ Chicken *yassa* is a favourite dish in the Gambia.

Id in the Gambia

In the Gambia, Muslim people celebrate Id-ul-Fitr by eating a special lunch dish, called *nyankantango*, which means 'ten types of food'. The dish includes smoked fish, rice, locust beans, groundnuts and palm kernel oil. Another favourite is chicken *yassa*, which is chicken in lemon juice. There is a recipe for chicken *yassa* on the opposite page. People also enjoy a sweet drink, called *ngalakh*, which is made from millet, groundnuts and fruit.

Chicken Yassa

EQUIPMENT
Lemon squeezer
Chopping knife
Chopping board
Large dish
Frying pan

INGREDIENTS

4 Chicken pieces

Juice of 2 lemons

1 Onion, chopped

Salt and pepper

3 Tablespoons of cooking oil

Cup of water

1 Pour the lemon juice over the chicken pieces. Then spread on the chopped onion and add the oil. Put this chicken mixture in the fridge.

2 Leave the chicken in the fridge for at least 2 hours. Then take the chicken pieces out of the sauce and ask an adult to brown them under a hot grill.

3 Separate the onions from the sauce through a sieve and fry them in the frying pan until they are soft. Add the sauce and cook for 5 minutes.

4 Add the chicken pieces, a cup of water and a little salt and pepper. Cover and simmer for 45 minutes. Add more water if necessary.

Always be careful with knives and hot pans. Ask an adult to help you.

17

Easter in Sierra Leone

Many people in West Africa, especially in the south, are Christians. Their religion, Christianity, was brought to West Africa by Europeans.

Easter is a Christian festival, which celebrates the time when Jesus came back to life after dying on the cross. In some countries, such as Nigeria, Ghana and Sierra Leone, Easter is a public holiday. In Freetown, the capital city of Sierra Leone, Easter is a very popular celebration. Families gather to spend time together.

▼ People leaving church on Easter Day, in Ghana.

Good Friday

After church on Good Friday, children make a life-sized rag doll from recycled materials. The doll represents Judas, who betrayed Jesus. Later, the doll is destroyed to show that Judas has been punished.

People do not eat meat on Good Friday, so dishes usually contain fish instead. The main meal of the day is called *olele*. This is a dish made from black-eyed beans, fish, pepper and onions, which is eaten with sweet potatoes and plantain. Another popular fish dish is fish pepper soup. There's a recipe for fish pepper soup on page 20.

This spicy fish ▶ pepper soup is often eaten on Good Friday.

Fish Pepper Soup

Chopping board
Chopping knife
Large saucepan
Cup

INGREDIENTS

500 g White, boneless fish, cut into cubes

4 Cups of water

2 Tomatoes

1 Onion, peeled

4 Sprigs of parsley

2 Chillies, chopped

2 Teaspoons of salt

1 Teaspoon of dried thyme

Ask an adult to chop the chillies for you. It is very painful if you get them in your eye or in a cut.

 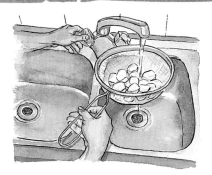

Wash the fish and place it in the saucepan with the water.

Finely chop the tomatoes, onions and parsley and add them to the fish with the chopped chillies.

Add the salt and thyme and stir.

Bring the soup to the boil, cover and simmer for 20 minutes.

Always be careful with hot pans and knives. Ask an adult to help you.

Easter Monday

Easter Monday is a fun day in Sierra Leone. It's 'picnic day', when many people pack a food hamper, along with a kite, and go to the beach. They fill the hamper with special food, which is too expensive to have every day. They might have chicken or crab, snapper or barracuda fish. These fish can be found in the seas around Freetown and are special favourites.

On the beach, people fly kites, enjoy their picnics or have a barbecue. Young people wander up and down the beach selling groundnuts and fruit such as mangoes and pineapples.

EASTER DAYS

Good Friday: The day Jesus was crucified

Easter Sunday: The day Jesus is believed to have risen from the dead.

Easter Monday: In most Christian countries, Easter Monday is a public holiday.

▼ Children selling snacks to the tourists on the beach in the Gambia.

Naming Ceremonies

From Nigeria to Senegal, people celebrate the naming of a baby with a special ceremony. Usually, this takes place when the baby is about a week old. It is an occasion for people to eat the best food they can afford.

Friends, family and important people in the village all gather together. Everyone whispers a special wish into the baby's ear. It might be 'Have a long life' or 'Be happy'.

▼ A baby's head is anointed with coconut in a naming ceremony in the Gambia.

Special food

The Yoruba people, who live in southern Nigeria, eat special food to represent different wishes for the baby. They pass round bowls of different foods and everyone has a small taste. They eat honey so that the baby will have a sweet life, palm oil so that his or her life will be smooth and easy, and salt so that his or her life will be interesting and tasty.

FIFTH BIRTHDAYS

In some countries, such as Nigeria, people have a special celebration on a child's fifth birthday. This is because many children die from diseases before they are five. So if a child reaches this age, it is seen as a big achievement.

▼ A basket of palm kernels (left) and oil made from them (right) in Sierra Leone.

Feast!

In Muslim communities there is a feast after the baby has been named. People eat goat meat. But first the meat is offered to the oldest man in the community, to show respect. Pounded yam with okra soup, or rice with pepper, or fried plantain are all popular dishes at naming ceremonies. There is a recipe for fried plantain on the opposite page.

▲ Plantain being grilled over hot charcoal, in Ghana.

WEIGHT IN GOLD

In the Gambia, sometimes a baby's head is shaved. The hair is weighed and the equivalent value in gold is given to the poor.

This baby belongs to the ▶ Wodaabe people, in Niger.

Fried Plantain

INGREDIENTS

4 Large plantain, or bananas
50 g Brown sugar
1 Teaspoon of cinnamon
50 g Butter or margarine

EQUIPMENT

Frying pan   Wooden spoon
Chopping board   Spatula
Knife

1 Peel the plantain or bananas and cut them in half lengthways.

2 Melt the butter in the frying pan. Add the sugar and half the cinnamon. Cook until the sugar has melted, stirring constantly.

3 Add the plantain or bananas, spoon the sugar mixture over them and fry for about a minute.

4 Use a spatula to put the plantain or bananas on a plate. Sprinkle the rest of the cinnamon on top.

Be careful when frying. Ask an adult to help you.

25

Yam Festivals

Yams are such an essential food that anyone who is good at growing them is thought to be a very important person. In Nigeria, Ghana and Sierra Leone, yam festivals are held in August, when the new yams are ready to be harvested. The period before the harvest is called the 'hungry months'. People living in towns try to return to their home villages to celebrate the yam festival.

▼ The seeds of yams are planted in mounds so that they can grow properly. The mounds keep the seeds cool and rain runs off.

Harvest

On the day of the yam festival, the women of each village get up very early and go to the fields to harvest the yams. They dig them out of the ground using hoes, and dust off the earth. Then they hold a short ceremony in the fields.

This Nigerian woman is ▶ deep-frying yams. Deep-fried yams are called *dunduns*.

The ceremony

Traditionally, people in Africa believe that their ancestors are very important. So when they have a successful harvest of yams, they thank their ancestors at the yam festival. The new yams are placed on a special stool and the ancestors are thanked with a short chant and with singing.

After the ceremony, a child is chosen to carry the new yams home. Then everyone rushes home to cook the new yams, along with other favourite dishes, such as fruit salads. There is a recipe for fruit salad on the opposite page.

People sing traditional songs of thanks and visit their friends. There is dancing and feasting late into the night.

Tasty fruit salads like ▶ this are eaten at the yam festival.

Fruit Salad

INGREDIENTS

4 Ripe mangoes
4 Bananas
1 Large tomato
1/2 Pineapple, cut into cubes

Juice from 1 lime
1 Cup of water
1 Cup of sugar
1 Cup of shredded coconut

EQUIPMENT

Chopping knife
Chopping board
Large bowl
Jug
Wooden spoon

Wash and peel the mangoes and chop them into bite-sized pieces. Peel and slice the bananas.

Cut the tomato in half, remove the seeds and cut it into cubes. Mix the tomato and all the fruit together in a large bowl.

In a jug, mix the lime juice with the water and sugar to make a dressing. Stir well.

Pour the dressing over the fruit, cover the bowl and put in the fridge for at least 1 hour. Sprinkle the shredded coconut on the top just before serving.

Always be careful with knives. Ask an adult to help.

Glossary

Ancestors Family members who died a long time ago.

Calabashes The dried and hollowed-out shells of gourds (a type of fruit), which are used as containers.

Crucified Put to death on a cross, as a punishment.

Fast To go without food for a period of time, often for religious reasons.

Grain The small, hard seed from various types of grasses, which people can cook and eat.

Harvest The collecting of grain, fruit and vegetables when they are ripe and ready to eat.

Nomads People who move from place to place to find food and water supplies.

Okra A type of vegetable with long, green pods.

Plantain A tropical fruit like a banana, but not so sweet.

Plantations Very large farms.

Preserve To treat food in a way that allows it to be kept for a long time before it is eaten.

Protein The essential part of a diet that helps us to grow.

Rain forests Thick forests that grow in the tropical areas of the world, where the climate is hot and very wet.

Winnowing Separating grain from the rest of the plant by tossing it into the air. The wind blows away the stalks and the heavier grain falls into the basket.

Author acknowledgements
The author would like to thank the following for their advice, support and information: Lucy Faemata Davies, Ivan Scott, Fenella White, Morounke Williams, Sam Woodhouse and the Marlborough Brandt Group.

Photograph and artwork acknowledgements
The publishers would like to thank the following for contributing to the pictures in this book:
Axiom *title page*/James H. Morris, 21/Steve J. Benbow, 22/James Morris; Antony Blake *contents page*, 27; Chapel Studios/Zul Mukhida 16, 19, 28; Robert Estall 24 (bottom)/Carol Beckwith; Eye Ubiquitous 5 (centre left)/Tim Durham, 8/Tim Durham; Hutchison 12, 18/Timothy Beddow; Impact 11/Giles Morley; Christine Osborne 14, 23; Panos *cover*/Ron Giling, 5(top left)/Betty Press, 5(bottom left)/Liba Taylor, 5(centre right)/Jeremy Hartley, 5(bottom right)/Ron Giling, 7/Betty Press, 9(top)/Liba Taylor, 9(bottom)/Jeremy Hartley, 10/Marcus Rose, 13/Marcus Rose, 26/Bruce Paton; Peter Sanders 6; Trip 24(bottom)/B. Seed; Wayland Picture Library 5 (top right), 15/James Morris.
Fruit and vegetable artwork is by Tina Barber. Map artwork on page 4 is by Hardlines.
Step-by-step recipe artwork is by Judy Stevens.

Topic Web and Resources

Food & Festivals TOPIC WEB

MATHS
Using and understanding data and measures (recipes).

Using and reading measuring instruments: scales.

Using weights and measures.

Using and understanding fractions.

SCIENCE
Food and nutrition.

Health.

Plants in different habitats.

Plants as a life process.

Separating mixtures of materials: sieving and dissolving.

Changing materials through heat.

GEOGRAPHY
Locality studies of West African countries.

Weather.

Farming.

Comparing physical landscapes.

Influence of landscape on human activities: farming and food festivals.

Migrations.

DESIGN AND TECHNOLOGY
Design a poster to advertise a food product.

Technology used in food production.

Packaging.

RE
Festivals

Islam

Christianity

African religions

ENGLISH
Make up a slogan to sell a food product.

Write a poem or story using food as the subject.

Write a menu you might find in a West African restaurant.

HISTORY
Colonialism and migrations to West Africa.

OTHER BOOKS TO READ

A Feast of Festivals by Hugo Slim (Pickering, 1996)

Celebrate Islamic Festivals by Khadijah Knight (Heinemann, 1997)

Celebrate Christian Festivals by Jan Thompson (Heinemann, 1997)

Festivals: Easter by Philip Sauvain (Wayland, 1997)

Festivals: Harvest by Clare Chandler (Wayland, 1997)

Festivals: Id-ul-Fitr by Kerena Merchant (Wayland, 1996)

Fiesta!: Nigeria by Paul Tessa (Watts, 1997)

This book meets the following specific objectives of the National Literacy Strategy's Framework for Teaching:

✓ Range of work in non-fiction: simple recipes (especially Year 2, Term 1), instructions, labels, captions, lists, glossary, index.

✓ Vocabulary extension: words linked to particular topics (food words) and technical words from work in other subjects (geography and food science).

Index

Page numbers in **bold** mean there is a photograph on the page.